Smart Investing Strategies

Maximize Your Wealth with Proven Techniques and Expert Tips

Vergil Long

loss due to the information herein, either directly or indirectly. Respective authors own all copyrights not held by the publisher. The information herein is offered for informational purposes solely, and is universal as so. The presentation of the information is without contract or any type of guarantee assurance. The trademarks that are used are without any consent, and the publication of the trademark is without permission or backing by the trademark owner. All trademarks and brands within this book are for clarifying purposes only and are the owned by the owners themselves, not affiliated with this document.

Table of Contents

Chapter 1

Introduction to Smart Investing

What is Smart Investing?

Smart investing is the practice of making informed and strategic financial decisions to maximize returns while minimizing risks. It's not about chasing quick profits or relying on luck; rather, it's a disciplined approach that requires understanding, patience, and careful planning. Smart investing involves analyzing different investment opportunities, assessing their potential risks and rewards, and aligning them with your financial goals.

At its core, smart investing is about making your money work for you. This means putting your capital into various financial instruments that have the potential to grow over time. The key is to choose investments that match your risk tolerance, time horizon, and financial objectives. This approach helps in building a diversified portfolio that can weather market fluctuations and provide steady returns.

One of the fundamental principles of smart investing is diversification. Diversification involves spreading your investments across different asset classes, such as stocks, bonds, real estate, and commodities. This strategy helps to reduce risk because if one investment performs poorly, others may perform well, balancing the overall portfolio. Diversification does not eliminate risk entirely, but it can significantly mitigate it.

Another critical aspect of smart investing is understanding the concept of risk versus reward. Every investment carries some level of risk, and higher potential returns usually come with higher risks. It's essential to assess how much risk you are willing to take and whether the potential reward justifies that risk. For instance, stocks generally offer higher returns than bonds, but they are also more volatile. A smart investor knows how to balance these factors to achieve their financial goals.

Financial literacy plays a vital role in smart investing. Understanding basic financial concepts and terminology can empower you to make better investment decisions. For example, knowing the difference between a stock and a bond, understanding how compound interest works, and being familiar with investment strategies like dollar-cost averaging can make a significant difference in your investment outcomes. Educating yourself continuously and staying updated with market trends and economic news can enhance your investment acumen.

Setting clear and achievable investment goals is another cornerstone of smart investing. Whether you're saving for retirement, buying a house, or funding your child's education, having specific goals can guide your investment strategy. It's important to set both short-term and long-term goals and create a plan to achieve them. This plan should include how much money you need to invest, the types of investments you will make, and the time frame for each goal. Regularly reviewing and adjusting your plan based on your progress and changes in your financial situation is crucial.

One common myth about investing is that it requires a large amount of money to get started. However, smart investing can begin with small amounts. Many investment platforms and financial institutions offer options for beginners with limited funds. For example, you can start investing in mutual funds or exchange-traded funds (ETFs) with relatively low initial investments. These investment vehicles provide diversification and professional management, making them suitable for novice investors.

Another misconception is that investing is too complicated for the average person. While the world of finance can seem daunting, many resources are available to help beginners learn and grow. Books, online courses, financial advisors, and investment clubs can provide valuable knowledge and support. The key is to start with the basics and gradually build your understanding. Over time, investing can become a more intuitive and manageable part of your financial life.

Setting up an emergency fund is an essential step before diving into investing. An emergency fund is a savings buffer that can cover unexpected expenses, such as medical emergencies, car repairs, or job loss. Having an emergency fund ensures that you don't have to dip into your investments prematurely, which can disrupt your long-term financial plan. Financial experts typically recommend keeping three to six months' worth of living expenses in an easily accessible account, such as a savings account.

Understanding your risk tolerance is another critical component of smart investing. Risk tolerance refers to your ability and willingness to endure market volatility and potential losses. It's influenced by various factors, including your financial situation, investment goals, time horizon, and psychological comfort with risk. Some people are more risk-averse and prefer safer investments like bonds, while others are more risk-tolerant and are comfortable investing in stocks. Knowing your risk tolerance helps you create a portfolio that aligns with your comfort level and financial objectives.

Smart investing also involves regular monitoring and rebalancing of your portfolio. Market conditions and your financial situation can change over time, affecting the performance and risk profile of your investments. Periodically reviewing your portfolio allows you to make necessary adjustments to maintain your desired asset allocation. Rebalancing involves selling some investments that have performed well and buying others that have underperformed to keep your portfolio in line with your original plan. This disciplined approach helps to manage risk and ensures that your investments remain aligned with your goals.

Tax efficiency is another important consideration in smart investing. Different investments are taxed differently, and understanding the tax implications of your investment choices can help you maximize your after-tax returns. For example, capital gains from the sale of stocks held for more than a year are typically taxed at a lower rate than short-term gains. Additionally, certain accounts, such as Individual Retirement Accounts (IRAs) and 401(k) plans, offer tax advantages that can help you save more for retirement. Consulting with a tax advisor or financial planner can help you develop a tax-efficient investment strategy.

Why Invest?

Investing is a crucial component of financial planning and wealth-building. It's not just for the wealthy or the financially astute; it's a fundamental practice that everyone should consider. The reasons for investing are manifold, ranging from building wealth to achieving financial independence, and even to securing a comfortable retirement. Understanding why investing is important can motivate you to start early and remain consistent, ultimately leading to financial security and the ability to meet your long-term goals.

One of the primary reasons to invest is to build and grow your wealth over time. While saving money in a traditional savings account is a good start, the interest earned is typically minimal and often fails to keep up with inflation. Investing, on the other hand, offers the potential for higher returns. By putting your money into stocks, bonds, mutual funds, or real estate, you can leverage the power of compound interest, which Albert Einstein famously referred to as the "eighth wonder of the world." Compound interest allows your earnings to generate even more earnings, creating a snowball effect that can significantly increase your wealth over time.

Investing also plays a critical role in achieving financial independence. Financial independence means having enough wealth to live off of without needing to work for money. This doesn't necessarily mean retiring early, although that can be a goal for some. Rather, it means having the freedom to make choices about how you spend your time, whether that's pursuing a passion, traveling, or simply having the peace of mind that comes with financial security. The earlier you start investing, the more time your money has to grow, and the sooner you can achieve financial independence.

Another compelling reason to invest is to outpace inflation. Inflation erodes the purchasing power of your money over time, meaning that the same amount of money will buy less in the future than it does today. Historically, the average annual inflation rate in the United States has been around 3%. To maintain your purchasing power and ensure that your money retains its value, you need to earn a return on your investments that exceeds the rate of inflation. Investing in a diversified portfolio of assets can help you achieve returns that outpace inflation, preserving and increasing your wealth over the long term.

Investing is also essential for funding major life goals and expenses. Whether you're saving for a down payment on a house, your children's education, or your own retirement, investing can help you reach these milestones more efficiently. For example, the cost of higher education has been rising steadily, and saving enough to cover these expenses can be challenging. By investing in a college savings plan, such as a 529 plan, you can take advantage of tax benefits and potential market growth to build a substantial education fund. Similarly, investing in retirement accounts like a 401(k) or an IRA allows you to benefit from tax advantages and compound growth, ensuring that you have enough saved to enjoy a comfortable retirement.

Diversification is another key reason to invest. Diversifying your investments means spreading your money across different asset classes, industries, and geographic regions to reduce risk. The idea is that if one investment performs poorly, others may perform well, balancing out your overall portfolio. This strategy helps to mitigate the impact of market volatility and reduces the risk of significant losses. A well-diversified portfolio can provide more stable returns over time, helping you to achieve your financial goals with less risk.

Investing also provides opportunities for passive income. Passive income is money earned from investments without active involvement. Examples include dividends from stocks, interest from bonds, rental income from real estate, and profits from business ventures in which you're a silent partner. Passive income can supplement your regular earnings, provide financial security, and even replace your primary source of income over time. Building a portfolio of income-generating investments can create a reliable stream of revenue that supports your financial needs and goals.

Moreover, investing can encourage better financial habits and discipline. When you commit to an investment plan, you often become more mindful of your spending and saving habits. Regularly contributing to your investment accounts requires budgeting and prioritizing your financial goals. This discipline can spill over into other areas of your financial life, helping you to save more, spend wisely, and make informed financial decisions.

Investing also allows you to take advantage of tax benefits. Many investment accounts offer tax advantages that can help you save money and grow your wealth more efficiently. For example, contributions to a traditional IRA or 401(k) are tax-deductible, reducing your taxable income for the year. Earnings in these accounts grow tax-deferred until you withdraw the money in retirement, potentially allowing you to save on taxes. Roth IRAs and Roth 401(k)s offer tax-free growth and tax-free withdrawals in retirement, providing significant tax advantages for long-term investors.

Lastly, investing can provide a sense of accomplishment and empowerment. Taking control of your financial future and watching your investments grow can be incredibly rewarding. It can boost your confidence, give you a sense of security, and provide the satisfaction of knowing that you are taking proactive steps to achieve your financial goals. The knowledge and experience gained through investing can also empower you to make better financial decisions and share your insights with others, contributing to a culture of financial literacy and empowerment.

The Importance of Financial Literacy

Financial literacy is the cornerstone of effective money management and long-term financial security. It encompasses understanding and applying various financial skills, including personal finance management, budgeting, investing, and understanding credit. Financial literacy empowers individuals to make informed decisions, avoid financial pitfalls, and achieve their life goals. In a world where financial products and markets are increasingly complex, financial literacy is not just beneficial but essential.

Imagine a young professional named Sarah. Fresh out of college, she lands her first job and starts receiving a steady paycheck. Without a solid understanding of financial principles, Sarah might fall into common traps: overspending, accumulating high-interest debt, and failing to save for the future. However, with a strong foundation in financial literacy, Sarah can navigate these challenges effectively. She can create a budget, manage her expenses, save and invest wisely, and plan for long-term goals like buying a home or retiring comfortably.

One of the primary benefits of financial literacy is the ability to create and stick to a budget. A budget is a financial plan that helps you allocate income towards expenses, savings, and investments. It provides a clear picture of your financial situation, enabling you to track where your money goes and make adjustments as needed. Without a budget, it's easy to overspend and find yourself living paycheck to paycheck. Financial literacy teaches you the importance of budgeting and provides the tools to create a realistic and effective budget.

Understanding credit and how it works is another critical aspect of financial literacy. Credit can be a powerful tool if used wisely, but it can also lead to significant financial problems if mismanaged. Financial literacy helps you understand the factors that affect your credit score, such as payment history, credit utilization, and length of credit history. It also teaches you how to use credit responsibly, avoid excessive debt, and maintain a good credit score. A strong credit score can open doors to favorable loan terms, lower interest rates, and better financial opportunities.

Investing is a key component of building wealth, and financial literacy provides the knowledge needed to make informed investment decisions. Many people shy away from investing due to a lack of understanding or fear of losing money. However, financially literate individuals understand the principles of investing, such as risk and return, diversification, and the importance of a long-term perspective. This knowledge enables them to create diversified investment portfolios that align with their risk tolerance and financial goals. By investing wisely, they can grow their wealth and achieve financial independence.

Financial literacy also encompasses understanding taxation and how to manage your tax liabilities effectively. Taxes are a significant expense for most people, and failing to understand the tax system can result in overpaying or facing penalties. Financially literate individuals know how to take advantage of tax deductions, credits, and retirement account benefits to minimize their tax burden. They also understand the importance of keeping accurate records and filing taxes on time. This knowledge can lead to significant savings and reduce the stress associated with tax season.

Another critical aspect of financial literacy is understanding the importance of emergency savings. Life is unpredictable, and unexpected expenses can arise at any time, such as medical emergencies, car repairs, or job loss. Without an emergency fund, you might have to rely on high-interest credit cards or loans to cover these expenses, which can lead to a cycle of debt. Financial literacy teaches you the importance of setting aside three to six months' worth of living expenses in a readily accessible account. This safety net can provide peace of mind and financial stability during challenging times.

Insurance is another area where financial literacy plays a crucial role. Insurance is designed to protect you from significant financial losses due to unforeseen events, such as accidents, illness, or natural disasters. However, understanding the different types of insurance, such as health, auto, home, and life insurance, can be complex. Financial literacy helps you evaluate your insurance needs, compare policies, and choose the right coverage for your situation. It also teaches you the importance of regularly reviewing and updating your insurance policies to ensure they continue to meet your needs.

Retirement planning is a long-term financial goal that requires a deep understanding of various financial concepts. Financial literacy equips you with the knowledge to estimate how much money you will need in retirement, understand different retirement accounts, such as 401(k)s and IRAs, and make informed decisions about saving and investing for retirement. It also helps you understand the benefits of starting early and taking advantage of compound interest. By being financially literate, you can create a comprehensive retirement plan that ensures you can maintain your desired lifestyle in your golden years.

Debt management is another critical skill gained through financial literacy. Debt can be a useful financial tool, but it can also become overwhelming if not managed properly. Financial literacy teaches you how to differentiate between good debt (such as a mortgage or student loan) and bad debt (such as high-interest credit card debt). It also provides strategies for paying off debt efficiently, such as the snowball or avalanche method, and teaches you how to avoid common debt traps. By managing debt effectively, you can improve your financial health and avoid the stress associated with excessive debt.

Financial literacy also promotes better financial decision-making. With a solid understanding of financial principles, you can evaluate different financial products and services, such as bank accounts, loans, and investment options, to determine which ones best meet your needs. You can also recognize and avoid financial scams and predatory lending practices. This ability to make informed decisions can save you money, protect your financial well-being, and help you achieve your financial goals more efficiently.

In addition to personal benefits, financial literacy has broader societal implications. A financially literate population is better equipped to participate in the economy, make informed voting decisions on financial policies, and contribute to overall economic stability. Financial literacy can also reduce the strain on social safety nets by enabling individuals to manage their finances independently and avoid financial crises.

To foster financial literacy, it's important to start education early. Financial literacy programs in schools can provide young people with the knowledge and skills they need to manage their finances effectively from a young age. Parents can also play a crucial role by teaching their children about money management and setting a positive example. For adults, there are numerous resources available, including books, online courses, workshops, and financial advisors, to help improve financial literacy.

Common Myths About Investing

Investing can seem daunting to beginners, largely because of the many myths and misconceptions that surround it. These myths can deter individuals from starting their investment journey, potentially costing them significant financial growth and security over time. Understanding and debunking these myths is crucial for anyone looking to build a solid investment portfolio and achieve their financial goals.

One of the most pervasive myths is that investing is only for the wealthy. This misconception stems from the idea that you need a large sum of money to begin investing. However, this is far from the truth. With the advent of technology and the rise of online brokerage platforms, it's easier than ever to start investing with small amounts. Many platforms allow you to open an account with no minimum balance and invest in fractional shares, meaning you can buy a portion of a stock rather than a whole share. This makes investing accessible to people of all income levels. The key is to start early and invest consistently, regardless of the amount.

Another common myth is that investing is akin to gambling. While both investing and gambling involve risk, they are fundamentally different activities. Gambling is based on chance and often involves short-term bets with high stakes. Investing, on the other hand, is about buying assets that have the potential to grow in value over time. It involves research, analysis, and strategic planning. Successful investors make informed decisions based on data and trends, and they understand the importance of diversification to mitigate risk. Unlike gambling, where the odds are often against you, investing offers the potential for long-term growth and wealth accumulation.

Many people believe that you need to be an expert to invest successfully. This myth can be intimidating for beginners, but the reality is that you don't need to be a financial wizard to start investing. Basic financial literacy and a willingness to learn are sufficient to get started. There are numerous resources available, from books and online courses to financial advisors and investment apps, that can help you understand the fundamentals of investing. Moreover, many investment platforms offer tools and educational materials to guide you through the process. The most important thing is to start and continue learning as you go.

The fear of losing money is another myth that keeps people from investing. While it's true that investing involves risk, the risk can be managed with a well-thought-out strategy. Diversification, which means spreading your investments across different asset classes and sectors, can help reduce the impact of a poor-performing investment. Additionally, investing with a long-term perspective allows you to ride out market volatility. Historically, the stock market has shown an upward trend over the long term, despite short-term fluctuations. By focusing on long-term goals and avoiding the temptation to react to short-term market movements, you can mitigate the risk of losses.

Some people believe that investing is too complicated and time-consuming. While it's true that some investment strategies can be complex, there are many simple and effective ways to invest without spending a lot of time. For instance, passive investing through index funds or exchange-traded funds (ETFs) is a straightforward approach that requires minimal time and effort. These funds track a specific market index and provide broad market exposure, making them an excellent choice for beginners. Additionally, automated investing services, or robo-advisors, can create and manage a diversified portfolio for you based on your risk tolerance and financial goals. This allows you to invest without needing to constantly monitor the market.

Another myth is that you need to constantly monitor your investments to be successful. This belief can create unnecessary stress and lead to impulsive decision-making. In reality, a hands-off approach can often be more effective. Once you have a well-diversified portfolio that aligns with your goals and risk tolerance, it's usually best to let your investments grow over time. Regularly reviewing your portfolio is important, but daily monitoring is not necessary. In fact, frequent trading based on short-term market movements can be detrimental to your overall returns due to transaction costs and potential tax implications.

Many people think that investing is only for the young. While it's true that starting to invest early gives your money more time to grow, it's never too late to begin. Even if you're closer to retirement, investing can still help you grow your wealth and protect against inflation. The key is to choose investments that match your time horizon and risk tolerance. For instance, older investors might opt for a more conservative portfolio with a higher allocation to bonds and dividend-paying stocks, which can provide income and stability. Regardless of your age, investing can help you achieve your financial goals and secure your future.

A common myth is that you need to follow the latest trends to be successful in investing. This belief can lead to chasing hot stocks or sectors, which can be risky and often results in disappointment. Successful investing is more about consistency and discipline than trying to time the market or pick the next big winner. Sticking to a well-diversified portfolio and regularly contributing to your investments is a more reliable strategy. It's also important to avoid the influence of market noise and hype, which can lead to emotional decision-making. Instead, focus on your long-term goals and the fundamentals of your investments.

Another misconception is that paying off debt should always take precedence over investing. While it's generally a good idea to pay off high-interest debt before investing, there are situations where it makes sense to do both simultaneously. For instance, if you have low-interest debt, it might be more beneficial to invest and take advantage of compound interest, especially if your investments have the potential to earn a higher return than the interest rate on your debt. Additionally, contributing to retirement accounts, especially if your employer offers a match, should be a priority. Balancing debt repayment and investing requires careful consideration of your financial situation and goals.

Finally, some people believe that they don't need to invest because they have a pension or expect Social Security to cover their retirement expenses. While these sources of income can be important components of your retirement plan, relying solely on them can be risky. Pensions are becoming less common, and the future of Social Security is uncertain. Moreover, these income sources might not be sufficient to maintain your desired lifestyle in retirement. Investing can provide additional income and help ensure that you have enough savings to cover your expenses and enjoy your retirement years. It's important to take control of your financial future and not rely solely on external sources.

Setting Your Investment Goals

Establishing clear investment goals is the foundation of a successful investment strategy. Without well-defined objectives, it's easy to lose focus, make impulsive decisions, or become discouraged by short-term market fluctuations. Defining what you aim to achieve through investing provides direction and helps in creating a structured plan that aligns with your financial aspirations.

When setting your investment goals, it's essential to start with a comprehensive evaluation of your current financial situation. This involves assessing your income, expenses, debts, and savings. Understanding your financial baseline allows you to determine how much you can realistically invest without compromising your day-to-day needs or emergency fund. It's important to maintain a balance between investing for the future and ensuring financial stability in the present.

One effective method for setting investment goals is to categorize them into short-term, medium-term, and long-term objectives. Short-term goals typically span one to three years and might include saving for a vacation, a down payment on a car, or an emergency fund buffer. Medium-term goals, which cover three to ten years, could involve saving for a home purchase, funding a child's education, or starting a business. Long-term goals often extend beyond ten years and generally focus on retirement planning, building substantial wealth, or leaving a legacy.

For example, consider Sarah, a 30-year-old professional. She decides to set her short-term goal as saving $10,000 within three years for a dream vacation. Her medium-term goal is to accumulate $50,000 over the next seven years for a down payment on a home. Lastly, her long-term goal is to build a retirement fund of $1 million by the age of 65. By clearly defining her goals, Sarah can tailor her investment strategy to meet these specific targets.

Once your goals are categorized, it's crucial to quantify them. Assigning a monetary value and a timeframe to each goal provides a clear target to work towards. This quantification helps you calculate the required investment returns and the amount you need to invest regularly. For instance, if Sarah wants to save $50,000 in seven years for a down payment, she can use an investment calculator to determine how much she needs to invest monthly, assuming an average annual return of 6%.

Understanding your risk tolerance is equally important when setting investment goals. Risk tolerance refers to your ability and willingness to endure market volatility and potential losses. This varies significantly from person to person, depending on factors such as age, income stability, investment experience, and psychological comfort with risk. A young investor like Sarah, with a longer time horizon until retirement, might have a higher risk tolerance compared to someone nearing retirement age. Assessing your risk tolerance ensures that your investment choices align with your comfort level and financial capacity.

Diversification is another key principle in setting and achieving your investment goals. Spreading your investments across different asset classes—such as stocks, bonds, real estate, and commodities— reduces risk and enhances the potential for returns. A diversified portfolio can cushion the impact of poor performance in any single investment. For instance, if the stock market experiences a downturn, gains in bonds or real estate can help offset losses. Diversification not only mitigates risk but also provides a balanced approach to achieving your financial objectives.

Regularly reviewing and adjusting your investment goals is vital to stay on track. Life circumstances, financial markets, and personal priorities can change, necessitating adjustments to your goals and strategies. Conducting an annual review of your investment portfolio and goals can help you make necessary changes to ensure you remain aligned with your overall financial plan. For example, if Sarah gets a significant salary increase, she might decide to allocate more funds towards her long-term retirement goal, potentially increasing her monthly contributions to her retirement account.

In addition to regular reviews, it's beneficial to stay informed about market trends and economic conditions. While it's not necessary to become an expert, having a basic understanding of market movements and how they impact your investments can help you make informed decisions. Subscribing to financial news, reading investment books, or attending seminars can enhance your knowledge and confidence in managing your investments. However, it's essential to avoid making impulsive decisions based on short-term market fluctuations; instead, focus on your long-term goals and strategy.

Setting realistic and achievable investment goals requires patience and discipline. It's easy to get swayed by stories of quick riches or high-risk, high-reward schemes, but such approaches often lead to disappointment and financial loss. Sticking to a well-thought-out plan and maintaining a long-term perspective increases your chances of success. For instance, the power of compound interest—earning returns on both your initial investment and the interest it generates—becomes more significant over time. By consistently investing and allowing your investments to grow, you can achieve substantial financial gains in the long run.

Automating your investments can also be a powerful tool in reaching your goals. Setting up automatic transfers from your bank account to your investment accounts ensures consistent contributions without the temptation to spend the money elsewhere. Many investment platforms offer automated investment plans, where funds are regularly invested in a diversified portfolio based on your risk tolerance and goals. Automation simplifies the investment process, promotes discipline, and helps you stay on course to achieve your financial objectives.

It's essential to consider the tax implications of your investment decisions. Different investments are taxed differently, and understanding these tax implications can help you optimize your returns. For instance, contributions to retirement accounts like 401(k)s or IRAs often come with tax advantages, such as tax-deferred growth or tax-free withdrawals in retirement. Tax-efficient investing strategies, such as holding investments for longer than a year to benefit from lower long-term capital gains tax rates, can also enhance your overall returns. Consulting with a tax advisor or financial planner can provide personalized advice tailored to your financial situation and goals.

Lastly, it's important to remember that investing is a journey, not a destination. Achieving your investment goals requires ongoing effort, learning, and adaptation. Celebrate your milestones along the way, whether it's reaching a savings target, achieving a certain rate of return, or simply sticking to your investment plan during turbulent times. These small victories can motivate you to stay committed to your long-term goals.

Chapter 2

Understanding the Basics

Types of Investments

Investing can seem like a complex and daunting endeavor, especially with the myriad of options available. Understanding the different types of investments is crucial for building a diversified portfolio that aligns with your financial goals and risk tolerance. Each investment type carries its own set of characteristics, benefits, and risks, which makes it essential to grasp their nuances to make informed decisions.

Stocks represent ownership in a company. When you purchase shares of a company's stock, you essentially buy a piece of that company. Stocks are known for their potential to provide high returns, but they also come with significant risk. The value of stocks can fluctuate widely based on the company's performance, market conditions, and broader economic factors. For example, consider an investor who bought shares in Amazon in its early days; their investment would have grown substantially as the company expanded and its stock price soared. However, investing in individual stocks requires careful research and monitoring, as the fortunes of a single company can change rapidly.

Bonds are debt securities issued by corporations, municipalities, or governments to raise capital. When you buy a bond, you are essentially lending money to the issuer in exchange for periodic interest payments and the return of the principal amount at maturity. Bonds are generally considered safer than stocks, but they offer lower potential returns. They are often used to preserve capital and generate steady income. For instance, U.S. Treasury bonds are viewed as virtually risk-free since they are backed by the full faith and credit of the U.S. government. Corporate bonds, on the other hand, carry higher risk and potentially higher returns, depending on the issuing company's creditworthiness.

Mutual funds pool money from multiple investors to purchase a diversified portfolio of stocks, bonds, or other securities. Managed by professional portfolio managers, mutual funds offer the benefit of diversification and professional management, making them a popular choice for individual investors. There are various types of mutual funds, including equity funds, bond funds, and balanced funds, each catering to different investment objectives and risk tolerances. For example, an equity mutual fund that invests in a broad range of stocks can provide exposure to the stock market without the need to pick individual stocks. However, mutual funds come with management fees that can impact overall returns.

Exchange-traded funds (ETFs) are similar to mutual funds but trade on stock exchanges like individual stocks. ETFs offer the flexibility of trading throughout the day at market prices, unlike mutual funds, which are priced at the end of the trading day. ETFs can track various indexes, sectors, commodities, or other assets, providing investors with diversified exposure to specific markets or investment themes. For instance, an investor looking to invest in the technology sector might choose an ETF that tracks the performance of a technology index. ETFs generally have lower expense ratios compared to mutual funds, making them a cost-effective investment option.

Real estate investment trusts (REITs) allow individuals to invest in large-scale, income-producing real estate. REITs own and operate a portfolio of real estate properties, such as office buildings, shopping centers, apartments, and hotels. They offer a way to invest in real estate without the need to buy, manage, or finance properties directly. REITs are required to distribute at least 90% of their taxable income to shareholders in the form of dividends, making them an attractive option for income-seeking investors. For example, a REIT specializing in commercial properties can provide regular income through rental payments while offering potential capital appreciation.

Commodities include physical assets such as gold, silver, oil, and agricultural products. Investing in commodities can provide a hedge against inflation and diversify a portfolio beyond traditional stocks and bonds. Commodity prices are influenced by supply and demand dynamics, geopolitical events, and economic conditions. For instance, gold is often viewed as a safe-haven asset during times of economic uncertainty or inflation. Investors can gain exposure to commodities through direct ownership, commodity-focused ETFs, or futures contracts. However, commodities can be highly volatile and require a thorough understanding of the market.

Cryptocurrencies have emerged as a new asset class, offering high potential returns but also significant risk. Cryptocurrencies like Bitcoin and Ethereum operate on decentralized networks using blockchain technology. They are known for their price volatility and speculative nature. While some investors view cryptocurrencies as a hedge against traditional financial systems and potential future currency, others see them as speculative assets with uncertain long-term value. Investing in cryptocurrencies requires a high risk tolerance and a willingness to navigate a rapidly evolving market.

Cash and cash equivalents, such as savings accounts, certificates of deposit (CDs), and money market funds, offer safety and liquidity. These investments are suitable for short-term goals or as a place to park funds during volatile markets. While they provide low returns, the principal is generally safe from market fluctuations. For example, a money market fund invests in short-term, high-quality debt securities and offers higher yields than a regular savings account while maintaining liquidity. Cash equivalents are an essential component of an emergency fund, ensuring that funds are readily available when needed.

Peer-to-peer (P2P) lending platforms connect borrowers with individual lenders, bypassing traditional financial institutions. Investors can earn interest by lending money to individuals or small businesses through these platforms. P2P lending offers the potential for higher returns compared to traditional savings accounts or bonds, but it also carries higher risk. The default rate of borrowers can impact returns, making it important to diversify across multiple loans. For instance, an investor might lend small amounts to numerous borrowers to spread the risk and increase the chances of earning a consistent return.

Collectibles, such as art, antiques, and rare coins, offer an alternative investment avenue. These tangible assets can appreciate in value over time and provide a hedge against inflation. Investing in collectibles requires specialized knowledge and expertise to identify valuable items and understand market trends. For example, rare stamps or vintage wines can become more valuable with age and rarity, offering potential capital appreciation. However, the market for collectibles can be illiquid, and the value can be subjective, depending on demand and collector interest.

Venture capital and private equity involve investing in early-stage companies or private businesses. These investments offer the potential for substantial returns but come with high risk. Venture capital funds provide capital to startups with high growth potential, while private equity firms invest in established companies to improve their operations and profitability. These investments require significant capital and a long-term commitment, as it can take years for a company to mature and generate returns. For instance, investing in a promising tech startup might yield significant returns if the company becomes successful, but it also carries the risk of failure.

Risk vs. Reward

Investing is a balancing act between the potential for reward and the accompanying risk. Understanding this dynamic is crucial for making informed investment decisions and building a portfolio that aligns with your financial goals and risk tolerance. The relationship between risk and reward is fundamental in finance, where higher potential returns usually come with greater risk. This chapter delves into the intricacies of risk versus reward, providing practical advice to help you navigate this essential aspect of investing.

Risk, in the context of investing, refers to the possibility of losing some or all of the invested capital. Different types of investments carry varying levels of risk. For example, stocks are generally considered riskier than bonds because their prices can be more volatile and are influenced by a wide range of factors, including company performance, market sentiment, and economic conditions. Conversely, bonds, particularly government bonds, are seen as safer but typically offer lower returns. Understanding the specific risks associated with different asset classes helps investors make more informed choices.

Reward, on the other hand, is the potential financial gain from an investment. This gain can come in the form of capital appreciation, dividends, interest payments, or a combination of these. Historically, stocks have offered higher average returns compared to bonds and cash equivalents, but they also come with higher volatility. For instance, an investor who bought shares of Apple a decade ago would have seen substantial growth in their investment, reflecting the high reward associated with the company's success. However, this potential for high reward is accompanied by significant risk, as evidenced by the stock market's fluctuations during economic downturns.

One of the key concepts in managing risk and reward is diversification. By spreading investments across different asset classes, sectors, and geographic regions, investors can reduce the impact of any single investment's poor performance on their overall portfolio. Diversification helps mitigate risk by ensuring that not all investments are affected by the same economic or market events. For example, an investor with a diversified portfolio of stocks, bonds, real estate, and commodities is less likely to experience significant losses compared to someone who invests solely in technology stocks.

Another important strategy for managing risk is asset allocation. This involves determining the appropriate mix of different asset classes in your portfolio based on your risk tolerance, investment goals, and time horizon. For example, a younger investor with a longer time horizon and higher risk tolerance might allocate a larger portion of their portfolio to stocks, which have higher growth potential but also higher volatility. In contrast, an older investor nearing retirement might prefer a more conservative allocation with a greater emphasis on bonds and cash equivalents to preserve capital and generate steady income.

Risk tolerance is a personal measure of how much risk an individual is willing and able to take. It is influenced by various factors, including financial goals, investment time horizon, income, and psychological comfort with market fluctuations. Assessing your risk tolerance is crucial for making investment decisions that you can stick with over the long term. For instance, if you are highly risk-averse, you might prefer investments with lower volatility, even if it means accepting lower returns. Conversely, if you have a higher risk tolerance, you might be willing to endure short-term market swings for the potential of higher long-term gains.

Emotional responses to market movements can significantly impact investment decisions. Fear and greed are two powerful emotions that can lead to irrational investment behavior. During market downturns, fear can drive investors to sell their investments at a loss, while greed can lead to chasing high returns during market upswings, often resulting in buying high and selling low. Maintaining a disciplined investment approach and sticking to a well-thought-out plan can help mitigate the influence of emotions. For example, implementing a systematic investment plan, such as dollar-cost averaging, can help smooth out the impact of market volatility and reduce the temptation to make impulsive decisions.

Understanding the different types of risks associated with investments is essential for managing them effectively. Market risk, also known as systematic risk, is the risk of losses due to factors that affect the entire market, such as economic recessions, political instability, or natural disasters. Diversification cannot eliminate market risk, but it can help mitigate its impact. Specific risk, or unsystematic risk, is associated with individual companies or industries and can be reduced through diversification. For instance, investing in a broad range of stocks from different sectors can reduce the impact of a poor-performing company on your portfolio.

Inflation risk is another important consideration. Inflation erodes the purchasing power of money over time, meaning that the real value of your investment returns can be diminished if they do not outpace inflation. Investments that provide a hedge against inflation, such as stocks, real estate, and commodities, can help protect your portfolio from this risk. For example, owning real estate can provide rental income that typically increases with inflation, while commodities like gold often appreciate in value when inflation rises.

Interest rate risk affects the value of fixed-income investments, such as bonds. When interest rates rise, the prices of existing bonds typically fall, as new bonds are issued with higher yields. Conversely, when interest rates decline, existing bonds with higher yields become more valuable. Understanding the relationship between interest rates and bond prices is crucial for managing this risk. For instance, an investor holding long-term bonds might face significant price volatility due to interest rate changes, while those holding short-term bonds might experience less impact.

Liquidity risk refers to the difficulty of selling an investment at its fair market value. Investments in less liquid assets, such as real estate or certain alternative investments, can be challenging to sell quickly without potentially accepting a lower price. Ensuring that a portion of your portfolio is invested in liquid assets, such as stocks and bonds, can help manage liquidity risk and provide access to funds when needed.

Credit risk, or default risk, is the risk that a bond issuer will be unable to make interest or principal payments. This risk is higher for corporate bonds

compared to government bonds. Assessing the
creditworthiness of bond issuers and diversifying
across different issuers and sectors can help mitigate
credit risk. For example, investing in a mix of high-
quality corporate bonds and government bonds can
provide a balance between higher yields and lower
default risk.

Diversification: The Key to Smart Investing

Diversification stands as one of the most crucial
principles in the realm of investing, often referred to
as the only free lunch in finance. By spreading
investments across various asset classes, sectors, and
geographical regions, investors can significantly
reduce risk while optimizing potential returns. This
strategy not only mitigates the impact of poor
performance from any single investment but also
capitalizes on the different growth patterns of
various assets. Understanding and implementing
diversification is essential for creating a robust and
resilient investment portfolio.

Imagine a farmer who plants only one type of crop.
If a disease strikes that specific crop, the farmer risks
losing the entire harvest. However, if the farmer
grows a variety of crops, the likelihood of total loss
diminishes, as the disease may not affect all types of

crops equally. Similarly, in investing, placing all your money in one stock or sector can lead to significant losses if that particular investment performs poorly. Diversifying your investments across different assets can help cushion against such downturns.

At its core, diversification involves mixing a variety of investments within a portfolio. This mix can include stocks, bonds, real estate, commodities, and cash equivalents. Each asset class responds differently to market conditions, and their prices do not move in tandem. For instance, when stock prices fall, bond prices often rise, providing a counterbalance to your portfolio. This interaction between different asset classes helps smooth out returns and reduces overall risk.

A well-diversified portfolio typically includes a mix of domestic and international stocks. Investing in international markets exposes your portfolio to growth opportunities outside your home country, which can be particularly beneficial if your domestic market is underperforming. For example, while the U.S. stock market might be experiencing a downturn, the European or Asian markets could be thriving. By diversifying globally, you can tap into growth potential in different regions, thereby enhancing your portfolio's performance.

Sector diversification is another critical aspect. Different sectors of the economy, such as technology, healthcare, finance, and consumer goods, often perform differently under various economic conditions. For instance, during an economic expansion, consumer discretionary stocks might perform well as people spend more. Conversely, during a recession, consumer staples and healthcare stocks might outperform, as people still need essential goods and services. By investing across multiple sectors, you reduce the risk of being overly exposed to any single economic trend.

Bond diversification is equally important. Bonds can be categorized by issuer (government, municipal, corporate), credit quality (investment grade, high yield), and maturity (short-term, intermediate, long-term). Government bonds are generally considered safer but offer lower returns, while corporate bonds provide higher yields but come with increased risk. Spreading investments across various bonds can help balance the need for income and safety.

Real estate investments add another layer of diversification. Real estate often has a low correlation with stocks and bonds, meaning its performance does not directly depend on the movements of these traditional asset classes. Investing in real estate can provide steady income through rental payments and potential for capital appreciation. Additionally, real estate investment trusts (REITs) offer a way to invest in real estate without the need to directly purchase and manage properties.

Commodities, such as gold, silver, oil, and agricultural products, can also play a role in a diversified portfolio. Commodities often act as a hedge against inflation and economic uncertainty. For example, gold prices typically rise during times of economic turmoil, providing a safety net when stock markets are volatile. Including a small allocation to commodities can enhance the overall stability of your portfolio.

While diversification helps mitigate risk, it is essential to avoid over-diversification. Holding too many investments can dilute potential returns and make portfolio management cumbersome. Striking the right balance between diversification and concentration is key. A well-constructed portfolio might include a mix of 20 to 30 different investments, which is generally sufficient to achieve diversification benefits without becoming unwieldy.

Rebalancing is a critical component of maintaining a diversified portfolio. Over time, the performance of different investments will cause your portfolio's asset allocation to drift from its original targets. For instance, if stocks perform exceptionally well, they might grow to constitute a larger portion of your portfolio, increasing your overall risk exposure. Periodic rebalancing involves selling some of the better-performing assets and reinvesting the proceeds into underperforming ones to realign your portfolio with your desired asset allocation. This disciplined approach helps manage risk and ensures that your portfolio remains aligned with your investment goals.

Tax considerations also play a role in diversification. Different investments are subject to various tax treatments, and strategic allocation can help optimize after-tax returns. For example, placing tax-efficient investments, such as index funds, in taxable accounts and holding tax-inefficient investments, like bonds, in tax-advantaged accounts (IRAs, 401(k)s) can improve your overall tax efficiency. Consulting with a tax advisor can provide personalized guidance on the most effective ways to structure your diversified portfolio.

Diversification is not a one-time task but an ongoing process. Regularly reviewing and adjusting your portfolio in response to changing market conditions, personal circumstances, and financial goals is crucial. Life events such as retirement, marriage, or purchasing a home may necessitate adjustments to your investment strategy. Staying informed about market trends and economic developments can help you make timely decisions to maintain diversification and manage risk effectively.

Incorporating diversification into your investment strategy requires discipline, patience, and a long-term perspective. It involves making calculated decisions based on thorough research and understanding of different asset classes. Avoiding the temptation to chase short-term gains or react impulsively to market fluctuations is vital. Instead, focus on building a well-diversified portfolio that aligns with your risk tolerance, time horizon, and financial objectives.

The Role of Time in Investing

Time is a crucial factor in the world of investing, often determining the success or failure of an investment strategy. Its importance cannot be overstated, as it influences everything from risk tolerance to compound interest and market fluctuations. Understanding the role of time in investing can help you make more informed decisions and build a portfolio that aligns with your financial goals.

Imagine you are planting a tree. In the first few years, it might not show much growth, but as time goes by, it starts to flourish, providing shade and fruit. Similarly, investments need time to grow and deliver returns. This growth is often driven by compound interest, one of the most powerful concepts in finance. Compound interest allows your investments to earn returns on both the principal amount and the accumulated interest over time. The longer you let your investments compound, the more significant the growth will be.

Consider the example of two investors, Alice and Bob. Alice starts investing $200 a month at the age of 25 and continues until she is 35, then stops but leaves her investments untouched. Bob starts investing $200 a month at the age of 35 and continues until he is 65. Assuming both achieve an average annual return of 7%, who ends up with more money at the age of 65? Surprisingly, Alice, who invested for only 10 years, ends up with more money than Bob, who invested for 30 years. This example underscores the power of starting early and letting time work in your favor.

Time also plays a critical role in determining your risk tolerance. Generally, the longer your investment horizon, the more risk you can afford to take. Young investors with decades ahead of them can usually endure short-term market volatility because they have time to recover from downturns. On the other hand, those nearing retirement might prioritize preserving capital over seeking high returns, as they have less time to recover from potential losses. Your investment strategy should therefore align with your time horizon, balancing growth with risk management.

Market fluctuations are another aspect where time significantly impacts investing. Stock markets are inherently volatile, with prices moving up and down based on various factors. In the short term, these fluctuations can be nerve-wracking, but over the long term, markets tend to trend upwards. Historical data shows that while the stock market can experience significant drops in any given year, it has consistently delivered positive returns over extended periods. By staying invested and not panicking during market downturns, you can benefit from the long-term growth of the markets.

The concept of dollar-cost averaging is closely tied to time and can be a valuable strategy for investors. Dollar-cost averaging involves regularly investing a fixed amount of money regardless of market conditions. This approach reduces the impact of market volatility, as you buy more shares when prices are low and fewer shares when prices are high. Over time, this can lead to a lower average cost per share and potentially higher returns. It also instills a disciplined investing habit, preventing emotional decision-making based on short-term market movements.

Rebalancing your portfolio is another time-sensitive activity that helps manage risk and maintain your desired asset allocation. As investments grow at different rates, your portfolio's asset allocation can drift from its original targets. Regularly reviewing and rebalancing your portfolio ensures that it remains aligned with your risk tolerance and investment goals. This might involve selling over-performing assets and reinvesting in under-performing ones, which can be emotionally challenging but is essential for maintaining a balanced portfolio.

Time also affects the tax implications of your investments. Different types of investments are subject to varying tax treatments, and the length of time you hold an investment can influence the amount of tax you pay. For instance, in many jurisdictions, long-term capital gains—profits from selling assets held for more than a year—are taxed at a lower rate than short-term capital gains. Understanding these tax implications can help you make more tax-efficient investment decisions, ultimately enhancing your after-tax returns.

Retirement planning is a prime example of how time influences investing. Saving for retirement requires a long-term perspective, often spanning several decades. The earlier you start saving for retirement, the more time your investments have to grow, thanks to compound interest. Additionally, starting early allows you to make smaller, consistent contributions rather than needing to save large amounts later in life. This not only makes the process more manageable but also reduces financial stress as you approach retirement age.

Time also allows for the possibility of learning and adapting your investment strategy. As you gain experience and knowledge, you can refine your approach, making adjustments based on what you have learned. This ongoing education and adaptation can improve your investment outcomes over time. It's important to stay informed about market trends, economic developments, and new investment opportunities to make well-informed decisions.

However, it's equally important to avoid the pitfalls of market timing. Trying to predict market movements and timing your investments accordingly is notoriously difficult and often counterproductive. Even professional investors struggle to consistently time the market. Instead, focus on a long-term investment strategy that aligns with your financial goals and risk tolerance. Staying invested through market cycles and avoiding the temptation to make impulsive decisions based on short-term market movements is crucial.

Patience is a virtue in investing, and time rewards those who remain disciplined and committed to their investment strategy. Emotional reactions to market fluctuations can lead to poor decision-making, such as selling investments during a downturn out of fear. By maintaining a long-term perspective and trusting in your investment plan, you can navigate market volatility and stay on track towards your financial goals.

Diversification is another strategy closely linked to time. Over long periods, different asset classes, sectors, and regions can perform differently. By diversifying your investments, you can reduce risk and enhance potential returns. This approach allows you to benefit from the growth of various investments while mitigating the impact of any single investment's poor performance. Time enables you to ride out the ups and downs of individual investments, leading to a more stable and resilient portfolio.

Basic Financial Terminology

Understanding basic financial terminology is essential for anyone venturing into the world of investing. These terms not only form the foundation of financial literacy but also help you make informed decisions and communicate effectively with financial professionals. By familiarizing yourself with these concepts, you can navigate the complexities of investing with greater confidence and clarity.

One of the most fundamental terms in finance is "asset." An asset is anything of value that can be owned and controlled to produce positive economic value. Assets can be tangible, like real estate and equipment, or intangible, like stocks and patents. In the context of investing, assets typically refer to financial instruments such as stocks, bonds, and mutual funds.

"Liability" is another crucial term, representing any financial obligation or debt that an individual or organization owes to another party. Liabilities can include loans, mortgages, and accounts payable. Understanding the difference between assets and liabilities is key to assessing an individual's or a company's financial health.

"Equity" represents ownership in an asset after all liabilities have been deducted. In a corporate context, equity refers to shareholders' ownership in the company, often measured in the form of stock. Equity is calculated as the difference between a company's total assets and its total liabilities. For individual investors, equity can also refer to the value of an asset, such as a home, minus any outstanding mortgage.

The term "diversification" is central to risk management in investing. Diversification involves spreading investments across various asset classes, sectors, and geographical regions to reduce risk. The idea is that a diversified portfolio is less likely to suffer significant losses because not all asset classes or sectors will decline simultaneously. This strategy helps smooth out returns over time and protects against the volatility of individual investments.

"Portfolio" refers to the collection of investments owned by an individual or institution. A well-constructed portfolio typically includes a mix of asset classes, such as stocks, bonds, and cash equivalents, tailored to the investor's risk tolerance, time horizon, and financial goals. Regularly reviewing and rebalancing your portfolio is essential to ensure it remains aligned with your investment strategy.

"Stock" represents ownership in a company and entitles the shareholder to a portion of the company's profits and assets. Companies issue stock to raise capital, and shares of stock can be bought and sold on stock exchanges. Stocks are considered equity investments and can offer significant growth potential, but they also come with higher risk compared to other asset classes.

"Bond" is a fixed-income instrument representing a loan made by an investor to a borrower, typically a corporation or government. Bonds pay periodic interest payments, known as coupon payments, and return the principal amount at maturity. Bonds are considered less risky than stocks but generally offer lower returns. They play a crucial role in diversifying a portfolio and providing steady income.

"Mutual fund" is an investment vehicle that pools money from multiple investors to purchase a diversified portfolio of securities. Mutual funds are managed by professional fund managers who aim to achieve specific investment objectives. They offer individual investors access to diversified portfolios without the need to buy and manage each security individually. Mutual funds come in various types, including equity funds, bond funds, and balanced funds, each with different risk and return profiles.

"Exchange-Traded Fund (ETF)" is similar to a mutual fund but trades on stock exchanges like individual stocks. ETFs offer the benefits of diversification and professional management, along with the flexibility of intraday trading. They often have lower fees compared to mutual funds and can be a cost-effective way to gain exposure to a broad range of asset classes and sectors.

"Dividend" refers to the distribution of a portion of a company's earnings to its shareholders. Dividends are typically paid in cash or additional shares of stock and provide investors with a regular income stream. Not all companies pay dividends, but those that do are often established firms with stable earnings. Dividend-paying stocks can be an attractive option for income-focused investors.

"Capital gain" is the profit realized from the sale of an asset, such as stock or real estate, when the selling price exceeds the purchase price. Capital gains can be short-term or long-term, depending on the holding period of the asset. Short-term capital gains, realized on assets held for one year or less, are typically taxed at higher rates than long-term capital gains, which apply to assets held for more than one year.

"Market capitalization" (or market cap) measures the total value of a company's outstanding shares of stock. It is calculated by multiplying the current share price by the total number of outstanding shares. Market cap categorizes companies into different sizes: small-cap, mid-cap, and large-cap. Each category has different risk and return characteristics, with small-cap stocks generally being more volatile but offering higher growth potential compared to large-cap stocks.

"Yield" represents the income generated by an investment, usually expressed as a percentage of the investment's current price. For bonds, yield is the annual interest payment divided by the bond's current price. For stocks, yield typically refers to the dividend yield, calculated as the annual dividend payment divided by the stock's current price. Yield is an important metric for income-focused investors, helping them assess the income-generating potential of different investments.

"Expense ratio" is a measure of the annual operating expenses of a mutual fund or ETF, expressed as a percentage of the fund's average net assets. The expense ratio includes management fees, administrative costs, and other operational expenses. Lower expense ratios are generally more favorable, as high expenses can erode investment returns over time. Comparing expense ratios is crucial when selecting mutual funds or ETFs to ensure you are getting good value for your investment.

"Asset allocation" refers to the process of dividing an investment portfolio among different asset classes, such as stocks, bonds, and cash, based on an investor's risk tolerance, time horizon, and financial goals. Asset allocation is a key determinant of a portfolio's risk and return characteristics. A well-balanced asset allocation strategy can help manage risk and achieve long-term investment objectives.

"Rebalancing" involves periodically adjusting the allocation of assets in a portfolio to maintain the desired level of risk and return. As different asset classes perform differently over time, a portfolio's asset allocation can drift from its original targets. Rebalancing involves selling over-performing assets and reinvesting in under-performing ones to restore the portfolio's target allocation. This disciplined approach helps manage risk and ensures the portfolio remains aligned with the investor's goals.

"Liquidity" refers to the ease with which an asset can be converted into cash without significantly affecting its price. Highly liquid assets, such as stocks of large companies and government bonds, can be quickly sold at market value. Illiquid assets, such as real estate and private equity, can take longer to sell and may require a price discount. Liquidity is an important consideration when constructing a portfolio, as it affects an investor's ability to access funds in times of need.

"Risk tolerance" is an individual's willingness and ability to endure fluctuations in the value of their investments. It is influenced by factors such as financial goals, time horizon, and personal comfort with volatility. Understanding your risk tolerance is essential for selecting appropriate investments and developing a portfolio that aligns with your financial objectives.

"Time horizon" refers to the length of time an investor expects to hold an investment before needing to access the funds. A longer time horizon allows for a greater ability to withstand market volatility and take on higher-risk investments with potentially higher returns. Conversely, a shorter time horizon may necessitate a more conservative investment approach to preserve capital and ensure funds are available when needed.

Chapter 3

Building a Strong Foundation

Creating a Financial Plan

Creating a financial plan is like charting a course for a long journey. Without a clear plan, you might find yourself adrift, making decisions that are reactive rather than proactive. A well-thought-out financial plan helps you set goals, manage risk, and allocate resources effectively, ensuring you stay on track to meet your life objectives.

The first step in creating a financial plan is to set clear and realistic financial goals. These goals should be Specific, Measurable, Achievable, Relevant, and Time-bound (SMART). Start by identifying short-term goals, such as building an emergency fund or paying off high-interest debt. Then, consider medium-term goals like saving for a down payment on a house or funding your children's education. Finally, outline long-term goals, such as retirement savings and estate planning. Writing down your goals can provide motivation and a sense of direction.

Once you have defined your goals, it's crucial to assess your current financial situation. Begin by calculating your net worth, which is the difference between your assets and liabilities. List all your assets, including cash, investments, real estate, and personal property. Then, list your liabilities, such as mortgages, car loans, student loans, and credit card debt. This snapshot of your financial health will help you understand where you stand and what needs to be addressed.

Next, track your income and expenses to create a clear picture of your cash flow. Detailed records of your monthly income from all sources, such as salary, bonuses, and investment income, are essential. Similarly, track all your expenses, categorizing them into fixed expenses (like rent or mortgage payments, utilities, and insurance) and variable expenses (such as groceries, entertainment, and dining out). This exercise helps identify areas where you can reduce spending and allocate more funds towards your financial goals.

With a clear understanding of your financial situation, you can create a budget. A budget is a powerful tool that helps you control your spending, save for the future, and ensure you are living within your means. Start by allocating funds for essential expenses and financial goals. Then, allocate money for discretionary spending. It's important to be realistic and flexible, allowing for occasional adjustments. Regularly reviewing and updating your budget will help you stay on track and make informed financial decisions.

Building an emergency fund is a critical component of any financial plan. An emergency fund acts as a safety net, providing financial security in case of unexpected expenses, such as medical emergencies, car repairs, or job loss. Aim to save at least three to six months' worth of living expenses in a liquid, easily accessible account. Having an emergency fund can prevent you from going into debt when unforeseen expenses arise and give you peace of mind.

Debt management is another vital aspect of financial planning. High-interest debt, such as credit card debt, can be a significant obstacle to achieving your financial goals. Prioritize paying off high-interest debt as quickly as possible, while making minimum payments on lower-interest debt. Consider strategies such as the avalanche method, which focuses on paying off debt with the highest interest rate first, or the snowball method, which targets smaller balances first to build momentum. Reducing and eventually eliminating high-interest debt frees up more money for savings and investments.

Saving and investing are essential for building wealth and achieving long-term financial goals. Start by establishing a regular savings habit, setting aside a portion of your income each month. Automating your savings can make this process easier and more consistent. Once you have built an emergency fund and paid off high-interest debt, focus on investing for the future. Diversify your investments across different asset classes, such as stocks, bonds, and real estate, to manage risk and maximize returns. Consider your risk tolerance, time horizon, and financial goals when choosing investments.

Retirement planning is a critical component of a comprehensive financial plan. Begin by estimating how much money you will need in retirement, taking into account factors such as your desired lifestyle, healthcare costs, and inflation. Contribute regularly to retirement accounts, such as a 401(k) or IRA, and take advantage of employer matches if available. The power of compounding can significantly grow your retirement savings over time, so the earlier you start, the better.

Insurance is an essential part of financial planning, providing protection against unforeseen events that could derail your financial goals. Evaluate your insurance needs and ensure you have adequate coverage for health, life, disability, and property. Life insurance can provide financial security for your dependents in case of your untimely death, while disability insurance can replace a portion of your income if you are unable to work due to illness or injury. Regularly review your insurance policies to ensure they continue to meet your needs as your circumstances change.

Estate planning is often overlooked but is a crucial element of a financial plan. It involves preparing for the management and distribution of your assets after your death. Start by creating a will that outlines your wishes and names an executor to carry them out. Consider establishing a trust to manage your assets and provide for your beneficiaries. Designate beneficiaries for your retirement accounts and insurance policies, and create a durable power of attorney and healthcare directive to ensure your wishes are respected if you become incapacitated. Consulting with an estate planning attorney can help you navigate this complex process and ensure your plans are legally sound.

Regularly reviewing and updating your financial plan is essential to stay on track and adapt to changes in your life. Major life events, such as marriage, the birth of a child, or a change in employment, can significantly impact your financial situation and goals. Schedule periodic reviews of your financial plan, at least annually, to assess your progress and make necessary adjustments. This proactive approach ensures that your financial plan remains relevant and effective in helping you achieve your goals.

Creating a financial plan is not a one-time event but an ongoing process that evolves with your life circumstances and goals. By setting clear objectives, assessing your financial situation, creating a budget, managing debt, and investing wisely, you can build a solid foundation for financial security and success. Regularly reviewing and adjusting your plan ensures that you stay on track and can confidently navigate the financial complexities of life.

Budgeting for Investments

Budgeting for investments requires a careful balance between managing daily expenses and setting aside funds for future growth. It's an approach that involves strategic planning, disciplined execution, and a deep understanding of your current financial situation. Investing is not just about selecting the right stocks or bonds; it begins with creating a solid budget that frees up capital to allocate towards your investment goals.

To start, it's essential to have a clear picture of your financial landscape. Begin by listing all sources of income, including your salary, bonuses, rental income, dividends, and any other earnings. This comprehensive view provides the foundation for understanding how much money you have at your disposal each month. Next, document all your expenses. Categorize them into fixed expenses, like mortgage or rent, utilities, insurance, and car payments, and variable expenses, such as groceries, entertainment, dining out, and travel. Tracking these expenses over a few months helps identify spending patterns and areas where you might cut back.

Once you have a clear understanding of your income and expenses, it's time to create a budget. The goal is to ensure that your essential expenses are covered while also setting aside money for investments. One effective method is the 50/30/20 rule. Allocate 50% of your income to necessities, 30% to discretionary spending, and 20% to savings and investments. This framework provides a balanced approach, ensuring that you are living within your means while also preparing for the future.

Building an emergency fund is a crucial step before diving into investments. An emergency fund acts as a financial buffer, covering unexpected expenses such as medical emergencies, car repairs, or sudden job loss. Aim to save at least three to six months' worth of living expenses in a high-yield savings account. This fund ensures that you won't need to liquidate your investments prematurely, which could result in losses or missed opportunities for growth.

After establishing an emergency fund, the next step is to allocate money specifically for investments. Determine a fixed percentage of your income that you can consistently set aside each month. Automating this process can help maintain discipline and ensure regular contributions to your investment accounts. For example, you might set up automatic transfers from your checking account to your brokerage account or retirement savings plan. This approach removes the temptation to spend the money elsewhere and fosters a habit of consistent investing.

Understanding your investment goals is vital in shaping your budgeting strategy. Are you saving for a short-term goal like a down payment on a house, or are you focused on long-term growth for retirement? Your goals will influence the types of investments you choose and the amount of risk you are willing to take. Short-term goals might require more conservative investments to preserve capital, while long-term goals can accommodate more volatility in pursuit of higher returns.

Diversifying your investment portfolio is another key element. Diversification spreads your risk across various asset classes, such as stocks, bonds, real estate, and commodities. By not putting all your eggs in one basket, you can mitigate the impact of poor performance in a single investment. Regularly review and rebalance your portfolio to maintain your desired asset allocation, especially as market conditions change.

It's also important to educate yourself about different investment options and strategies. Read books, attend seminars, follow financial news, and consider working with a financial advisor if needed. Understanding the basics of stocks, bonds, mutual funds, ETFs, and other investment vehicles enables you to make informed decisions that align with your financial goals and risk tolerance.

Tax planning plays a significant role in budgeting for investments. Different investment accounts offer various tax advantages. For example, contributions to a traditional IRA or 401(k) are often tax-deductible, reducing your taxable income for the year. However, withdrawals in retirement are taxed as ordinary income. Conversely, Roth IRA contributions are made with after-tax dollars, but withdrawals in retirement are tax-free. Understanding the tax implications of your investment choices can help you maximize your after-tax returns.

Monitoring and adjusting your budget regularly is crucial to staying on track. Life circumstances and financial goals can change, necessitating adjustments to your budget. Major life events, such as marriage, the birth of a child, or a significant increase in income, may require you to revisit your financial plan. Schedule regular reviews of your budget and investment strategy, at least annually, to ensure they remain aligned with your goals.

Avoiding lifestyle inflation is another important consideration. As your income increases, it's tempting to upgrade your lifestyle with more expensive cars, homes, or vacations. While it's natural to want to enjoy the fruits of your labor, it's also important to balance this with your long-term financial goals. Instead of allowing your expenses to rise in tandem with your income, maintain a modest lifestyle and channel the extra funds into your investment accounts.

Debt management is also integral to successful budgeting for investments. High-interest debt, such as credit card debt, can erode your financial stability and hinder your ability to invest. Prioritize paying off high-interest debt as quickly as possible. Once this debt is under control, you can focus on leveraging low-interest debt strategically, such as taking out a mortgage for real estate investments that appreciate over time.

Finally, stay disciplined and patient. Investing is a long-term endeavor, and the markets can be volatile. Stick to your budget and investment plan, avoiding the temptation to make impulsive decisions based on short-term market fluctuations. Regular investments, even in small amounts, can accumulate significantly over time thanks to the power of compounding. By maintaining a disciplined approach, you can navigate market ups and downs while steadily growing your wealth.

Setting Up an Emergency Fund

An emergency fund is the cornerstone of financial stability, acting as a buffer against life's unexpected expenses. Whether it's a sudden medical bill, car repair, or job loss, having a dedicated reserve of funds can prevent financial turmoil and keep you from spiraling into debt. Setting up an emergency fund involves strategic planning, disciplined saving, and a solid understanding of your financial needs.

The first step in establishing an emergency fund is to determine the appropriate size for your safety net. Financial experts typically recommend saving three to six months' worth of living expenses. This amount ensures that you can cover essential costs such as housing, utilities, groceries, and insurance, even if your income is suddenly interrupted. To calculate this, start by listing your monthly expenses. Include rent or mortgage payments, utility bills, groceries, transportation costs, insurance premiums, and any other regular expenses. Multiply this total by three to six, depending on your comfort level and job stability, to find your target emergency fund amount.

Once you have a target amount in mind, it's time to create a savings plan. Set a realistic timeline for building your emergency fund, taking into account your income and current financial obligations. Break down the total amount into manageable monthly contributions. For example, if your goal is to save $12,000 in two years, you would need to set aside $500 per month. This approach makes the task less daunting and helps you stay on track.

Automating your savings is a powerful way to ensure consistency. Set up automatic transfers from your checking account to a dedicated savings account each month. By doing this, you treat your savings like any other recurring bill, reducing the temptation to spend the money elsewhere. Choose a high-yield savings account for your emergency fund to maximize your interest earnings while keeping the funds easily accessible. Online banks often offer competitive interest rates and lower fees compared to traditional brick-and-mortar banks.

While building your emergency fund, it's important to identify and eliminate unnecessary expenses. Review your monthly spending habits and look for areas where you can cut back. Small changes, such as dining out less frequently, canceling unused subscriptions, or finding more affordable alternatives for entertainment, can add up over time. Redirect the money saved from these cutbacks into your emergency fund to accelerate your progress.

Another effective strategy is to allocate windfalls towards your emergency fund. Bonuses, tax refunds, and monetary gifts can provide a significant boost to your savings. Instead of using these unexpected funds for discretionary spending, deposit them directly into your emergency fund. This approach can help you reach your target amount faster without impacting your regular budget.

Creating a separate account specifically for your emergency fund is crucial. Mixing these funds with your regular checking or savings accounts can lead to accidental spending. A dedicated account ensures that the money is reserved solely for emergencies. Additionally, having a separate account makes it easier to track your progress and stay motivated as you watch your savings grow.

Maintaining an emergency fund requires ongoing discipline. Once you reach your target amount, resist the urge to dip into the fund for non-emergency expenses. It's essential to define what constitutes an emergency. True emergencies are unexpected, necessary, and urgent. For example, using the fund for a medical bill or car repair is justified, but tapping into it for a vacation or new gadget is not.

Regularly reviewing and adjusting your emergency fund is also important. Life circumstances change, and your financial needs may evolve. Annual reviews of your budget and expenses can help ensure that your emergency fund remains adequate. For instance, if you experience a significant increase in living expenses or take on new financial responsibilities, you may need to increase the size of your fund accordingly.

In addition to saving for emergencies, consider building multiple layers of financial security. For instance, having a health savings account (HSA) can help cover medical expenses, reducing the need to tap into your emergency fund. Similarly, maintaining proper insurance coverage, including health, auto, home, and disability insurance, can protect you from large, unexpected costs.

Building an emergency fund can be challenging, especially if you are also managing debt or other financial goals. It's important to strike a balance. While prioritizing debt repayment is crucial, allocating even a small amount towards your emergency fund each month can provide a sense of security. Start with a modest goal, such as saving $1,000, and gradually increase your target as your financial situation improves.

To stay motivated, track your progress visually. Use a savings tracker or app to monitor your contributions and watch your balance grow. Celebrating milestones, such as reaching 25%, 50%, or 75% of your goal, can provide a sense of achievement and encourage you to keep going. Sharing your progress with a trusted friend or family member can also provide accountability and support.

Involving the entire household in the savings effort can make the process more manageable and rewarding. Discuss the importance of an emergency fund with your partner or family members and set collective goals. Encourage everyone to contribute ideas for cutting expenses and finding additional ways to save. This collaborative approach can strengthen your financial habits and foster a shared commitment to achieving financial stability.

While setting up an emergency fund might seem daunting, the peace of mind it provides is invaluable. Knowing that you have a financial cushion to fall back on in times of need can alleviate stress and allow you to focus on other financial goals. It also prevents the need to rely on credit cards or loans, which can lead to debt and financial strain.

Understanding Your Risk Tolerance

Risk tolerance is a fundamental concept in the world of investing. It refers to an individual's ability and willingness to endure the fluctuations in the value of their investments. Understanding your risk tolerance is crucial because it influences the types of investments you choose, the allocation of assets in your portfolio, and ultimately, your overall investment strategy. Recognizing how much risk you can comfortably take on ensures that you remain invested during market downturns and stay on track to meet your financial goals.

Several factors contribute to an individual's risk tolerance, including financial situation, investment goals, time horizon, and personal comfort with uncertainty. A thorough assessment of these factors can provide a clearer picture of your risk tolerance, guiding you in making informed investment decisions.

One of the primary determinants of risk tolerance is your financial situation. This encompasses your income, expenses, savings, and overall net worth. Individuals with a stable income, substantial savings, and little debt are generally in a better position to take on higher risk compared to those with volatile income or significant financial obligations. A strong financial foundation acts as a safety net, allowing you to weather potential losses without jeopardizing your financial stability.

Investment goals also play a critical role in shaping your risk tolerance. Goals can be short-term, such as saving for a vacation or a down payment on a house, or long-term, like building a retirement nest egg or funding a child's education. Short-term goals typically require a more conservative approach to preserve capital, as there is less time to recover from potential losses. Conversely, long-term goals can accommodate higher risk because the extended time horizon allows for the possibility of greater returns and recovery from market downturns.

Time horizon is another essential factor. The length of time you plan to hold an investment before needing to access the funds impacts how much risk you can take. Younger investors with decades before retirement can afford to take on more risk because they have time to ride out market volatility. In contrast, individuals nearing retirement may prefer lower-risk investments to protect their accumulated wealth and ensure its availability when needed.

Personal comfort with uncertainty is a deeply individual aspect of risk tolerance. Some people are naturally more risk-averse, preferring stable, predictable returns even if it means lower potential gains. Others are more risk-seeking, willing to accept significant fluctuations in their investment value for the chance of higher returns. It's important to be honest with yourself about how you react to market volatility. If the thought of a 20% drop in your portfolio's value keeps you up at night, you may have a lower risk tolerance and should adjust your investment strategy accordingly.

Assessing your risk tolerance involves a combination of self-reflection and practical evaluation. One effective method is to complete a risk tolerance questionnaire. These tools, often provided by financial advisors or available online, ask a series of questions about your financial situation, investment goals, and reactions to hypothetical market scenarios. The results can offer valuable insights into your risk profile and help guide your investment choices.

Understanding your risk tolerance also involves recognizing the different types of investment risk. Market risk, also known as systematic risk, affects the entire market and cannot be diversified away. Examples include economic recessions, political instability, and changes in interest rates. On the other hand, unsystematic risk is specific to a particular company or industry and can be mitigated through diversification. Examples include a company's management decisions, product recalls, or industry regulations.

Inflation risk is another consideration, especially for long-term investors. Inflation erodes the purchasing power of money over time, meaning that your investments need to grow at a rate that outpaces inflation to maintain their real value. Historically, stocks have provided higher returns than bonds or cash, making them a common choice for combating inflation risk, despite their higher volatility.

Liquidity risk refers to the ease with which an investment can be converted into cash without significantly affecting its price. Investments in real estate, private equity, or certain bonds may offer attractive returns but can be difficult to sell quickly if you need access to cash. Balancing your portfolio with more liquid assets, such as publicly traded stocks or money market funds, can help manage liquidity risk.

Credit risk, or default risk, is the risk that a bond issuer will be unable to make interest or principal payments. This risk is more significant with lower-rated bonds, such as junk bonds, which offer higher yields to compensate for the increased risk. Understanding the credit ratings of your bond investments can help you gauge their level of risk.

Interest rate risk is particularly relevant for fixed-income investments. When interest rates rise, the prices of existing bonds typically fall, as newer bonds offer higher yields. This inverse relationship can impact the value of your bond holdings, especially if you need to sell before maturity. Diversifying your bond investments across different maturities, known as laddering, can help mitigate interest rate risk.

Currency risk, or exchange rate risk, affects investments in foreign assets. Fluctuations in currency exchange rates can impact the value of your international investments. Investors can manage this risk through currency hedging strategies or by diversifying their portfolio across different currencies.

Once you have a clear understanding of your risk tolerance and the various types of investment risk, the next step is to align your investment strategy accordingly. Asset allocation is a key component of this process. It involves spreading your investments across different asset classes—such as stocks, bonds, and cash—to balance risk and reward. A well-diversified portfolio can help smooth out returns and reduce the impact of any single investment's poor performance.

For example, if you have a high risk tolerance and a long time horizon, you might allocate a larger portion of your portfolio to stocks, which historically offer higher returns but with greater volatility. On the other hand, if you have a lower risk tolerance or a shorter time horizon, you might favor bonds and cash, which provide more stability and predictable returns.

Regularly reviewing and rebalancing your portfolio is essential to maintaining an asset allocation that aligns with your risk tolerance. Market movements can cause your portfolio's allocation to drift over time, potentially increasing your risk exposure. Periodic rebalancing involves selling overperforming assets and buying underperforming ones to restore your target allocation.

It's also important to stay informed and adaptable. As your financial situation, goals, and market conditions change, your risk tolerance may evolve. Life events such as marriage, the birth of a child, or nearing retirement can prompt a reassessment of your investment strategy. Keeping an open dialogue with a financial advisor can help you navigate these changes and adjust your portfolio accordingly.

Choosing the Right Investment Accounts

Choosing the right investment accounts is a critical step in your financial journey, as it can significantly impact your ability to grow wealth and achieve your long-term goals. With a myriad of options available, each suited to different needs and tax considerations, understanding the nuances of various accounts will help you make informed decisions.

The first account many people consider is the traditional Individual Retirement Account (IRA). This account offers tax-deferred growth, meaning you don't pay taxes on investment gains until you withdraw the money, typically in retirement. Contributions to a traditional IRA may be tax-deductible, which can reduce your taxable income for the year you contribute. However, withdrawals in retirement are taxed as ordinary income. Traditional IRAs are particularly beneficial if you expect to be in a lower tax bracket during retirement than you are now, making the tax deferral advantageous.

In contrast, a Roth IRA provides tax-free growth. Contributions are made with after-tax dollars, meaning there's no immediate tax benefit. However, qualified withdrawals in retirement are entirely tax-free, provided certain conditions are met. This can be particularly advantageous if you expect to be in a higher tax bracket in retirement or if you value the certainty of tax-free income later in life. Roth IRAs also offer flexibility, as contributions (but not earnings) can be withdrawn at any time without penalty, providing a backup emergency fund.

Employer-sponsored retirement plans, such as 401(k)s and 403(b)s, are powerful tools for building retirement savings. These plans allow for higher annual contribution limits than IRAs and often include employer matching contributions, effectively providing free money to boost your savings. Like traditional IRAs, contributions to these accounts are typically tax-deductible, and taxes on investment gains are deferred until withdrawal. Maximizing employer contributions should be a priority, as it significantly accelerates your savings growth.

For individuals who are self-employed or run small businesses, options like SEP IRAs, SIMPLE IRAs, and Solo 401(k)s provide robust retirement savings opportunities. SEP IRAs allow for high contribution limits relative to income, making them suitable for high-earning self-employed individuals. SIMPLE IRAs are easier to set up and administer than other plans, with mandatory employer contributions. Solo 401(k)s offer the highest potential contribution limits and the flexibility to make both employee and employer contributions.

Beyond retirement accounts, taxable brokerage accounts offer great flexibility and no contribution limits. These accounts are ideal for goals other than retirement, such as buying a home, funding education, or general wealth accumulation. While contributions to taxable accounts are not tax-deductible, and investment gains are subject to capital gains tax, they provide access to a wide range of investment options and no restrictions on withdrawals.

Health Savings Accounts (HSAs) are another valuable investment vehicle, particularly for those with high-deductible health plans. HSAs offer triple tax advantages: contributions are tax-deductible, investment gains grow tax-free, and withdrawals for qualified medical expenses are also tax-free. After age 65, withdrawals for non-medical expenses are taxed as ordinary income, similar to a traditional IRA, making HSAs a versatile tool for both healthcare costs and retirement savings.

Education savings accounts, such as 529 plans and Coverdell Education Savings Accounts (ESAs), are designed to help parents and grandparents save for a child's education expenses. Contributions to these accounts grow tax-free, and withdrawals used for qualified education expenses are also tax-free. 529 plans are particularly popular due to their high contribution limits and flexibility in changing beneficiaries, while Coverdell ESAs offer more investment options but lower contribution limits.

When selecting the right investment accounts, it's essential to consider your specific financial goals, time horizon, and tax situation. Diversifying across different account types can provide a balanced approach, optimizing tax benefits while offering flexibility for various needs. For example, combining a Roth IRA with a traditional 401(k) can hedge against future tax rate changes, providing both tax-deferred and tax-free income sources in retirement.

Understanding the rules and limits associated with each account type is crucial. Contribution limits, income eligibility, and withdrawal rules vary significantly and can affect your overall strategy. For instance, the ability to contribute to a Roth IRA phases out at higher income levels, while traditional IRAs have no income limits for non-deductible contributions. Additionally, early withdrawal penalties and required minimum distributions (RMDs) can impact your planning, making it important to be aware of these aspects.

Automating contributions to your investment accounts can streamline your saving process and ensure consistency. Setting up automatic transfers from your checking account to your retirement accounts, brokerage accounts, or HSAs can help you stay on track with your savings goals without needing to remember to make manual contributions.

It's also important to review and adjust your investment accounts periodically. Life changes such as a new job, marriage, or the birth of a child can necessitate changes in your savings strategy. Regularly reviewing your accounts can ensure that your contributions are optimized, your asset allocation remains appropriate, and you're taking full advantage of any employer matching contributions or tax benefits.

Consulting with a financial advisor can provide personalized guidance tailored to your unique situation. An advisor can help you navigate complex decisions, optimize your account choices, and create a comprehensive financial plan that aligns with your goals. They can also assist in tax planning, ensuring that you're making the most of available tax advantages and minimizing your tax liability.

While choosing the right investment accounts might seem daunting initially, breaking it down into manageable steps can simplify the process. Start by identifying your primary financial goals, whether they are retirement savings, education funding, or general wealth accumulation. Next, explore the various account types that align with these goals, considering the tax implications, contribution limits, and flexibility each offers. Finally, implement a strategy that balances these factors, automating contributions and reviewing your plan regularly to stay on track.

Chapter 4

Stock Market Investing

Introduction to Stocks

Stocks represent ownership in a company, and investing in them can be a powerful way to build wealth over time. Understanding stocks and how they work is essential for anyone looking to navigate the world of investing. Imagine you own a small part of a business. If that business grows and becomes more valuable, so does your share. This is the essence of investing in stocks.

When you buy a stock, you purchase a share in a company. This share represents a fraction of ownership in that company. Companies issue stocks to raise capital, which they can use to grow their business, develop new products, or pay off debt. In return, investors receive a claim on the company's assets and earnings. If the company performs well, the value of your shares may increase, and you can sell them for a profit. Additionally, some companies pay dividends, which are portions of their profits distributed to shareholders.

There are two main types of stocks: common stocks and preferred stocks. Common stocks are the most widely held and traded type of stock. Owners of common stocks have voting rights, usually one vote per share, which allows them to influence corporate decisions like electing the board of directors. On the other hand, preferred stocks typically do not offer voting rights but provide a fixed dividend, making them more like a bond. Preferred shareholders are also prioritized over common shareholders when it comes to dividends and asset liquidation in case of bankruptcy.

To buy stocks, you need to open a brokerage account. This account acts as an intermediary between you and the stock market. Online brokerages have made it easier and more affordable for individuals to invest in stocks, with many offering zero-commission trades. Once your account is set up and funded, you can start buying and selling stocks. It's important to research and understand the companies you're investing in. Look at their financial statements, business models, competitive advantages, and market conditions.

The stock market can be volatile, with prices fluctuating due to various factors such as economic data, corporate earnings reports, political events, and market sentiment. This volatility can be both an opportunity and a risk. For example, during a market downturn, stock prices may drop significantly, offering a chance to buy shares at a lower price.

Conversely, prices can also rise quickly, providing opportunities to sell for a profit. It's crucial to stay informed and be prepared for these fluctuations.

Investing in stocks is often part of a broader strategy to diversify your portfolio. Diversification involves spreading your investments across various asset classes, such as bonds, real estate, and commodities, to reduce risk. Within the stock portion of your portfolio, you can diversify by investing in companies of different sizes, sectors, and geographic regions. This way, if one stock or sector performs poorly, the impact on your overall portfolio is minimized.

There are several strategies for investing in stocks, each with its own approach to risk and return. One common strategy is value investing, where you look for undervalued stocks that are trading below their intrinsic value. This strategy involves analyzing financial statements, assessing a company's future growth prospects, and determining its fair value. If you believe a stock is undervalued, you buy it with the expectation that the market will eventually recognize its true worth, leading to a price increase.

Another popular strategy is growth investing, which focuses on companies with high growth potential. These companies may not be profitable yet but are expected to grow rapidly due to their innovative products or services, expanding market share, or other competitive advantages. Growth stocks can offer substantial returns but also come with higher risk, as their success often depends on future performance and market conditions.

Income investing is a strategy that prioritizes generating regular income from your investments. This approach often involves investing in dividend-paying stocks, which provide a steady income stream. Dividend stocks can be particularly attractive for retirees or those seeking passive income. However, it's important to evaluate the sustainability of a company's dividend payments and its overall financial health.

Another strategy is index investing, which involves buying shares of an index fund or exchange-traded fund (ETF) that tracks a specific stock market index, such as the S&P 500. This approach provides broad market exposure, diversification, and lower fees compared to actively managed funds. Index investing is a passive strategy, meaning you're not trying to pick individual stocks but rather investing in the overall market.

While investing in stocks can be lucrative, it's not without risks. Market risk, also known as systematic risk, affects all stocks and is influenced by factors like economic conditions, interest rates, and geopolitical events. Company-specific risk, or unsystematic risk, pertains to individual companies and their operations, such as management decisions, product recalls, or regulatory issues. Diversifying your portfolio can help mitigate these risks, but it's important to be aware of them and manage your investments accordingly.

Long-term investing is often recommended for those looking to build wealth through stocks. The stock market has historically trended upward over the long term, despite short-term volatility. By holding onto your investments for several years or even decades, you can benefit from compounding returns. Compounding occurs when your investment gains generate additional earnings, which are then reinvested to produce even more gains. This snowball effect can significantly boost your wealth over time.

It's also essential to have a clear investment plan and stick to it. Determine your financial goals, risk tolerance, and time horizon before investing. Your goals might include saving for retirement, buying a home, or funding your children's education. Your risk tolerance is your ability to withstand market fluctuations and potential losses. Your time horizon is the period you plan to hold your investments before needing the money. These factors will help you choose the right stocks and investment strategy.

Regularly reviewing your portfolio is crucial to ensure it aligns with your goals and risk tolerance.

Market conditions and your personal circumstances can change, requiring adjustments to your investments. Rebalancing your portfolio periodically can help maintain your desired asset allocation and risk level. This process involves selling some investments that have performed well and buying others that haven't to keep your portfolio balanced.

Lastly, emotional discipline is key to successful stock investing. It's easy to get caught up in market hype or panic during downturns, but making impulsive decisions based on emotions can lead to poor outcomes. Stay focused on your long-term goals and stick to your investment plan, even during market turbulence. Remember that investing is a marathon, not a sprint, and patience can be one of your greatest assets.

How to Analyze Stocks

Analyzing stocks requires a blend of art and science, as it involves both quantitative and qualitative assessments to determine the potential value and performance of a company's shares. For beginners, this process might seem daunting, but breaking it down into manageable steps can make it more approachable and less intimidating. The goal is to make informed decisions based on a thorough understanding of a company's financial health, business model, competitive landscape, and market conditions.

Start with fundamental analysis, which focuses on evaluating a company's financial statements. The three main financial statements to examine are the income statement, balance sheet, and cash flow statement. The income statement provides insight into a company's profitability over a specific period, showing revenues, expenses, and net income. Look for growing revenues and consistent profit margins, which indicate a healthy, expanding business. The balance sheet offers a snapshot of the company's financial position at a given point in time, detailing assets, liabilities, and shareholders' equity. A strong balance sheet typically has more assets than liabilities, suggesting financial stability. The cash flow statement reveals how cash is generated and used in operations, investments, and financing activities. Positive cash flow from operations is a good sign, as it shows the company can generate sufficient cash to sustain and grow its business.

Next, consider key financial ratios derived from these statements to get a clearer picture of the company's performance. The price-to-earnings (P/E) ratio compares the current share price to the company's earnings per share, providing a gauge of how much investors are willing to pay for a dollar of earnings. A high P/E ratio might indicate that the stock is overvalued, while a low P/E ratio could suggest it is undervalued. The price-to-book (P/B) ratio compares the market value of the company's shares to its book value, which is the value of its assets minus liabilities. This ratio helps assess whether the stock is fairly priced, undervalued, or overvalued based on the company's net assets.

The return on equity (ROE) measures a company's profitability by comparing net income to shareholders' equity. A high ROE indicates efficient use of equity capital to generate profits. The debt-to-equity (D/E) ratio evaluates a company's financial leverage by comparing its total debt to shareholders' equity. A lower ratio suggests a more financially stable company with less reliance on borrowed money. The current ratio, which compares current assets to current liabilities, assesses the company's ability to meet short-term obligations. A ratio above 1 indicates good short-term financial health.

Beyond the numbers, qualitative analysis plays a crucial role in understanding a company's potential. Investigate the company's business model and competitive advantages. A strong business model with a clear value proposition and a sustainable competitive advantage, such as proprietary technology, strong brand recognition, or a large network of customers, can provide a solid foundation for long-term growth. Assess the company's management team, as effective leadership is critical for executing business strategies and navigating challenges. Look for experienced executives with a track record of success in the industry.

Industry analysis is another vital component. Understand the industry dynamics and how the company fits within its sector. Consider factors like market size, growth potential, barriers to entry, and competitive landscape. Companies operating in rapidly growing industries with high barriers to entry and limited competition often have better prospects. However, even in competitive industries, companies with unique strengths or innovative approaches can thrive.

Macroeconomic factors also influence stock performance. Analyze broader economic conditions, such as interest rates, inflation, and economic growth, which can impact a company's operations and profitability. For example, high-interest rates might increase borrowing costs, affecting companies with significant debt. Similarly, economic downturns can reduce consumer spending, impacting companies reliant on discretionary spending.

Once you have gathered and analyzed all this information, it's essential to synthesize it into a cohesive investment thesis. An investment thesis is a concise summary of why you believe a stock is a good investment based on your analysis. It should outline the company's strengths, potential growth drivers, and any risks or challenges it might face.

Risk assessment is a critical part of the analysis. Every investment carries risk, and understanding the specific risks associated with a stock can help you make better decisions. Consider factors like market risk, which affects all stocks, and company-specific risks, such as management changes, product recalls, or regulatory issues. Evaluate the company's ability to withstand these risks and its strategies for mitigating them.

Technical analysis, while often used in conjunction with fundamental analysis, focuses on studying price movements and trading patterns. Technical analysts use charts and indicators to identify trends and potential entry or exit points for stocks. Common tools include moving averages, which smooth out price data to identify trends, and relative strength index (RSI), which measures the speed and change of price movements to identify overbought or oversold conditions.

Lastly, keep an eye on market sentiment and news. Investor sentiment can significantly influence stock prices, sometimes causing them to deviate from their fundamental values. Stay informed about news affecting the company, its industry, and the broader market. Major events like earnings reports, product launches, or regulatory changes can impact stock prices.

Understanding Stock Market Indices

Stock market indices serve as barometers of market performance, providing a snapshot of the overall health and direction of the market. They represent the collective movement of selected stocks and are essential tools for investors, analysts, and economists alike. Understanding how these indices work and their significance can greatly enhance your ability to navigate the stock market.

A stock market index is essentially a statistical measure that tracks the performance of a specific group of stocks. These groups can be based on various criteria, such as company size, industry, or geographic location. For instance, the S&P 500 index includes 500 of the largest publicly traded companies in the United States, spanning various industries. This diversity allows the S&P 500 to serve as a robust indicator of the overall U.S. stock market.

Indices are constructed using different methodologies. The most common types are price-weighted, market capitalization-weighted, and equal-weighted indices. A price-weighted index, such as the Dow Jones Industrial Average (DJIA), gives more weight to stocks with higher prices. This means that a significant price change in a high-priced stock will have a more substantial impact on the index than a similar change in a lower-priced stock. The DJIA includes 30 large, publicly-owned companies based in the U.S., and its movements are often seen as reflective of the broader economy.

Market capitalization-weighted indices, like the S&P 500 and the NASDAQ Composite, assign weights based on the market value of each company's outstanding shares. In these indices, larger companies have more influence. This method ensures that the index reflects the market value of the companies it includes, providing a more accurate representation of the market's overall performance. For example, a significant movement in a tech giant like Apple or Microsoft will significantly impact the S&P 500 due to their large market capitalizations.

Equal-weighted indices give each stock the same weight, regardless of its price or market capitalization. This approach offers a different perspective, as it treats all companies equally, regardless of size. An example of this is the S&P 500 Equal Weight Index, which often provides insights into the performance of smaller companies within the S&P 500, offering a more balanced view.

Understanding the components and weighting of an index is crucial because it affects how the index behaves. A market heavily influenced by a few large companies can see significant swings based on the performance of those companies alone. Conversely, in an equal-weighted index, movements are more evenly distributed, providing a different type of market insight.

Indices also serve various functions for different market participants. For investors, they are benchmarks against which to measure the performance of individual stocks or portfolios. If your portfolio outperforms the index, it indicates that your investment choices are yielding better-than-average results. Conversely, underperforming the index suggests that your investments may not be keeping pace with the broader market.

Indices also play a critical role in the creation of index funds and exchange-traded funds (ETFs). These investment vehicles aim to replicate the performance of a specific index by holding the same stocks in the same proportions. This approach provides investors with a way to gain broad market exposure without having to pick individual stocks. Index funds and ETFs are popular due to their diversification, lower costs, and simplicity compared to actively managed funds.

Market indices are not static; they are periodically reviewed and adjusted to reflect changes in the market and economy. Companies may be added or removed based on criteria like market capitalization, liquidity, and financial health. For example, a company experiencing significant growth might be added to the S&P 500, while another facing decline might be removed. These adjustments help ensure that indices remain relevant and accurately represent the segments of the market they are designed to track.

Indices can also be categorized by the specific markets or sectors they represent. For example, the Russell 2000 index focuses on small-cap companies in the U.S., providing insights into the performance of smaller businesses. Sector-specific indices, such as the NASDAQ-100 Technology Sector Index, track the performance of companies within a particular industry, offering a targeted view of that sector's health and trends.

Global indices provide a broader perspective on international markets. The MSCI World Index, for instance, includes stocks from 23 developed countries, offering a comprehensive view of global market performance. Similarly, the FTSE All-World Index covers both developed and emerging markets, allowing investors to gauge the overall direction of the global economy.

For investors looking to diversify internationally, understanding global indices is essential. These indices can highlight economic trends and shifts in different regions, helping investors make more informed decisions about where to allocate their assets. They also provide a way to compare the performance of domestic markets against global benchmarks, offering additional context for investment strategies.

Market indices are also influenced by economic indicators and events. For example, changes in interest rates, inflation data, employment reports, and geopolitical events can all impact stock prices and, consequently, the indices that track them. Understanding the relationship between these factors and market indices can provide valuable insights for predicting market movements and making strategic investment decisions.

Despite their utility, it's important to recognize that indices have limitations. They can be influenced by outliers—companies whose extreme performance skews the overall index. Moreover, indices may not fully capture the nuances of market performance, such as the impact of smaller companies or specific sectors. Therefore, while indices are valuable tools, they should be used in conjunction with other forms of analysis and research.

The Role of Dividends

Dividends are a central component of the investment landscape, representing a tangible return on investment for shareholders. These periodic payments from companies to their shareholders can be a crucial element in the overall return of an investment portfolio. Understanding the role of dividends requires an exploration of their various types, the rationale behind them, their impact on investor behavior, and their significance in different market conditions.

Firstly, it's essential to comprehend the different forms dividends can take. The most common type is the cash dividend, which is a direct payment to shareholders, typically distributed quarterly. Companies may also offer stock dividends, where additional shares are provided instead of cash. Stock dividends can indicate a company's confidence in its growth prospects, although they don't immediately provide liquidity to investors. Special dividends are another category, paid on an irregular basis, often resulting from extraordinary profits or asset sales. These are usually one-off payments and may not be a reliable income source for investors seeking regular returns.

The rationale behind paying dividends is multifaceted. For established companies with stable cash flows, dividends are a way to distribute excess profits to shareholders, signaling financial health and stability. They can also act as a tool for attracting and retaining investors, particularly those seeking income, such as retirees. Dividends provide a clear indicator of a company's profitability and its ability to generate cash flow, which can be especially appealing during periods of economic uncertainty. For companies, consistent dividend payments can build trust and credibility in the market, contributing to a positive perception among investors and analysts.

Dividends also play a significant role in investor behavior. Many investors rely on dividend income as a steady revenue stream, which becomes particularly important in low-interest-rate environments where other fixed-income investments may offer diminished returns. Dividend-paying stocks can provide a buffer against market volatility, as the income generated can help mitigate losses during downturns. Investors often view dividend-paying stocks as less risky, given that these companies are typically more mature and financially stable. This perception can lead to a 'dividend premium,' where stocks of companies that pay dividends trade at higher valuations compared to non-dividend-paying counterparts.

The impact of dividends on total return should not be underestimated. Historical data has shown that dividends constitute a substantial portion of long-term equity returns. Reinvesting dividends can significantly enhance the compounding effect, leading to greater wealth accumulation over time. For example, an investor who reinvests dividends buys additional shares with the dividend payments, which in turn generate more dividends in the future. This cycle of reinvestment can dramatically increase the value of an investment portfolio over decades, particularly in a tax-advantaged account where dividends are not immediately taxable.

Market conditions influence the significance of dividends in different ways. During bull markets, when stock prices are rising, capital gains may overshadow the importance of dividends. However, in bear markets or periods of economic stagnation, dividends can provide a crucial source of return when capital appreciation is hard to come by. High-dividend-yield stocks often become more attractive in such scenarios, offering a degree of safety and a guaranteed return component. Furthermore, in inflationary environments, dividends can act as a hedge. Companies that consistently increase their dividends often do so at a rate that outpaces inflation, thereby preserving the purchasing power of the income generated.

It's also important to consider the tax implications of dividends. In many jurisdictions, dividends are taxed at a different rate than capital gains. Qualified dividends in the United States, for example, are taxed at a lower rate than ordinary income, providing a tax-efficient income stream for investors. However, the tax treatment can vary significantly depending on the investor's country of residence and the type of account in which the dividends are held. Tax considerations can influence an investor's preference for dividend-paying stocks versus growth stocks, which may offer higher potential returns but with different tax implications.

The policy decisions of companies regarding dividends are influenced by their financial health, growth prospects, and strategic goals. Companies in the growth phase may prefer to reinvest profits back into the business rather than paying out dividends. This reinvestment can fund expansion, research and development, and other projects aimed at increasing future profitability. On the other hand, mature companies with limited growth opportunities often return a larger portion of their earnings to shareholders through dividends. This decision-making process can be guided by the desire to maintain a certain dividend payout ratio, which is the percentage of earnings paid out as dividends. A stable or growing dividend payout ratio can signal management's confidence in the company's future earnings.

Dividend policy can also be influenced by external factors, such as economic conditions and regulatory changes. For instance, during economic downturns, companies may cut or suspend dividends to conserve cash, which can negatively impact stock prices and investor sentiment. Conversely, regulatory changes that favor dividend taxation can encourage companies to increase dividend payments. Shareholder preferences and activism can also play a role, as institutional investors and activist shareholders might push for higher dividends if they believe excess cash is not being utilized efficiently.

Investors need to assess the sustainability of dividends when evaluating dividend-paying stocks. A high dividend yield might appear attractive, but it can sometimes be a red flag if it's not supported by the company's earnings and cash flow. The payout ratio is a key metric in this assessment. A payout ratio significantly above 100% suggests that a company is paying out more in dividends than it is earning, which is typically unsustainable in the long run. Investors should also consider the company's debt levels, as high debt can strain cash flows and jeopardize future dividend payments.

Common Stock Market Strategies

Investing in the stock market can seem daunting at first, but understanding common market strategies can help demystify the process and provide a clear path to potentially profitable investments. These strategies range from conservative approaches aimed at preserving capital to aggressive tactics designed to maximize returns. Each strategy has its own set of principles, risk levels, and potential rewards, catering to different investor goals and temperaments.

One of the most fundamental strategies is buy and hold, which involves purchasing stocks and holding them for an extended period, regardless of short-term market fluctuations. The rationale behind this approach is that over time, the stock market tends to rise, driven by economic growth and corporate profitability. By holding onto investments for the long term, investors can benefit from compound growth and avoid the pitfalls of trying to time the market. This strategy requires patience and a steadfast belief in the long-term potential of chosen investments. Historical data supports the efficacy of buy and hold, showing that despite periodic downturns, the stock market has generally trended upward over decades.

Contrasting with the buy and hold strategy is active trading, where investors frequently buy and sell stocks to capitalize on short-term market movements. Active traders often use technical analysis, studying past price movements and trading volumes to predict future trends. This strategy requires significant time, effort, and expertise, as it involves constant monitoring of the market and quick decision-making. While active trading can potentially yield high returns, it also carries higher risks and transaction costs, which can erode profits if not managed carefully.

Another popular strategy is value investing, which involves identifying undervalued stocks that are trading below their intrinsic value. Value investors believe that the market sometimes misprices stocks due to overreactions to news or short-term issues. By purchasing these undervalued stocks, investors hope to profit when the market eventually recognizes the stock's true value. This approach often requires thorough fundamental analysis, examining a company's financial statements, earnings, management quality, and competitive position. Legendary investors like Warren Buffett have popularized value investing, demonstrating its potential for significant long-term gains.

Growth investing, on the other hand, focuses on companies that exhibit high potential for future growth, even if their current valuations are high. Growth investors seek out companies with strong revenue and earnings growth, innovative products or services, and a competitive edge in their industry. These companies often reinvest their earnings to fuel further growth rather than paying dividends. While growth stocks can offer substantial returns, they also come with higher volatility and risk, as their success often hinges on continued strong performance and market conditions.

Dividend investing is a strategy that targets stocks paying regular dividends, providing investors with a steady income stream. Dividend-paying stocks are often seen as less volatile and more stable, making them attractive to conservative investors, such as retirees. This strategy involves evaluating the dividend yield, payout ratio, and the company's ability to sustain and grow its dividend payments. Reinvesting dividends can also enhance returns through compounding, where the dividends generate additional income over time.

Index investing involves purchasing shares in index funds or exchange-traded funds (ETFs) that replicate the performance of a specific market index, such as the S&P 500. This strategy offers broad market exposure, diversification, and lower costs compared to actively managed funds. Index investing is based on the efficient market hypothesis, which suggests that it is difficult to consistently outperform the market through stock picking or market timing. By mirroring the performance of a market index, investors can achieve market-average returns with minimal effort and lower risk.

Contrarian investing is a strategy where investors go against prevailing market trends by buying stocks that are out of favor and selling those that are popular. Contrarians believe that the market often overreacts to news and events, leading to mispriced securities. By taking positions opposite to the crowd, contrarian investors aim to profit from the eventual correction of these mispricings. This strategy requires a strong conviction and the ability to withstand potential short-term losses, as going against the consensus can be challenging and risky.

Sector rotation is a strategy that involves shifting investments among different sectors of the economy based on their performance in various economic cycles. For example, during an economic expansion, cyclical sectors like consumer discretionary and technology might perform well, while defensive sectors like utilities and healthcare might be more resilient during a recession. By anticipating economic trends and adjusting their portfolio accordingly, investors can potentially enhance returns and reduce risk.

Momentum investing capitalizes on the continuance of existing market trends. Momentum investors believe that stocks that have performed well in the recent past are likely to continue performing well in the near future. This strategy involves identifying and investing in stocks with strong upward price momentum while avoiding or shorting those with downward momentum. While momentum investing can yield significant profits, it also carries risks, as trends can reverse unexpectedly, leading to potential losses.

Dollar-cost averaging is a strategy where investors regularly invest a fixed amount of money into a particular stock or fund, regardless of its price. This approach reduces the impact of market volatility by spreading out purchases over time, potentially lowering the average cost per share. Dollar-cost averaging is particularly useful for investors without a large lump sum to invest and for those who wish to mitigate the risk of investing a significant amount at an inopportune time. This disciplined approach encourages consistent investing and can build wealth steadily over the long term.